# Mountain Flora

## Weeds or Wildflowers

by Marlynn D. Mulder

**DORRANCE**
PUBLISHING CO
EST. 1920
PITTSBURGH, PENNSYLVANIA 15238

Dorrance Publishing Co
585 Alpha Drive
Pittsburgh, PA 15238
Visit our website at *www.dorrancebookstore.com*

ISBN: 978-1-4809-3383-5
eISBN: 978-1-4809-3360-6

Every year when the white frozen winter releases its grip on the land, many dormant plants start to grow. The warmth of the sun and the moisture from the melted snow creates a wonderful display. Here you will find a compilation of some of my favorites. From early spring blooms, to late summer blossoms, I would like to dedicate this collection to my wonderful husband. He has endured countless hours of waiting for me and wondering where I disappeared while trying to get the perfect picture. Flora in the Colorado mountains are always a sight that gives lasting memories. So, I leave this for you to decide; weeds or wildflowers?

Marlynn D. Mulder

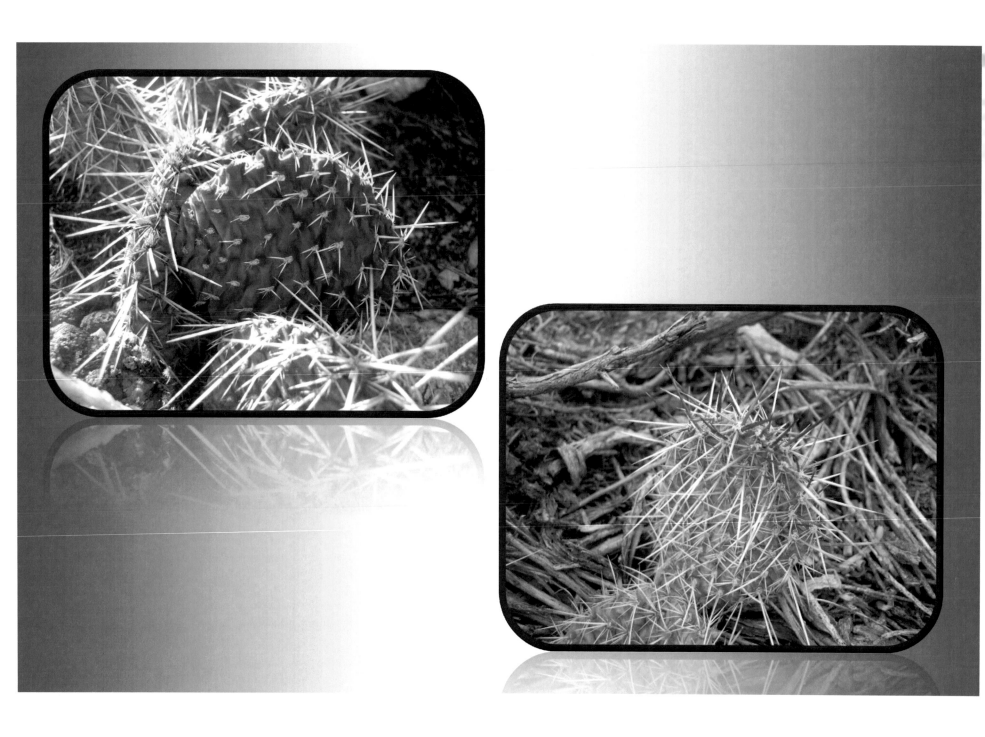